100 MTM TIPS
FOR THE PHARMACIST

100 MTM TIPS FOR THE PHARMACIST

Marsha K. Millonig, BPharm, MBA

American Pharmacists Association®
Improving medication use. Advancing patient care.

APhA   Washington, D.C.

Acquiring Editor: Sandra J. Cannon
Managing Editor: Paula Novash
Copyeditor: Mary DeAngelo
Graphic Designer: Michele Danoff, Graphics By Design
Cover Design: Mariam Safi, APhA Creative Services
Proofreader: Amy Morgante
Indexer: Suzanne Peake
Editorial Assistance: Kellie Burton

© 2009 by the American Pharmacists Association

Published by the American Pharmacists Association
1100 15th Street, NW, Suite 400
Washington, DC 20005-1707
www.pharmacist.com

To comment on this book via e-mail, send your message to the
publisher at aphabooks@aphanet.org

Library of Congress Cataloging-in-Publication Data

Millonig, Marsha K.
  100 MTM tips for the pharmacist / Marsha K. Millonig.
    p. ; cm.
  ISBN 978-1-58212-107-9
1. Communication in pharmacy. 2. Patient education. 3.
Pharmacy—Practice. I. American Pharmacists Association. II. Title.
III. Title: One hundred MTM tips for the pharmacist.
  [DNLM: 1. Medication Therapy Management—United States. 2.
Pharmaceutical Services—trends—United States. 3.
Pharmacy—trends—United States. 4. Professional
Practice—trends—United States. QV 737 M656z 2008]

  RS56.M55 2008
  615'.1068--dc22

                        2008032800

Life is change. Growth is optional.
Choose wisely.

Karen Kaiser Clark

TABLE OF CONTENTS

Chapter 4 Physician/Pharmacist Collaborative Relationships

Chapter 5 Documenting Services

Chapter 6 Payment, Billing, and Reconciliation

Chapter 12 Continuing Professional Education and Skills Development

Chapter 13 Patient Care Tips

Chapter 14 MTM Models and Resources

FOREWORD

Have you ever thought about where good ideas come from and how they evolve? In an article from *Inc.* magazine, October 2002, Anne Stuart asked, "Where Do Great Ideas Come From?" For many entrepreneurs, it's not from books or market research, it's from keeping their eyes and ears open to possibilities. Many products available today came from one person who had a problem and wondered how many people out there were facing the same issue. A good example of this is the FlavorX™ system that we now find in over 30,000 pharmacies worldwide. Examples such as these beg the question, "Why didn't I think of that?"

Unfortunately, the trials and tribulations of daily work usually prevent us from recognizing good ideas when they present themselves—even when they are right in front of us. Even in moments of true inspiration, we become overwhelmed when we think about how to implement such an idea. As a result, we don't pursue opportunities that can create better services and improve the health of patients. Knowing this, it becomes imperative that we consciously open our minds to the possibility of an idea, ask more questions, and then take a risk on an idea that can potentially help us achieve our goals.

Medication Therapy Management (MTM) services was born out of the need to help patients make better use of medications. Although this may sound basic, implementing solutions that address this need has required pharmacists to develop many practical ideas to bring awareness of MTM services to patients and create value within our health care system.

In this book, many contributors—from pharmacists to academicians to technicians—share ideas that they have successfully implemented in their practices. The value of this book lies in the combined experience of its contributors and the thoughts and questions that it will provoke in your mind as you create plans for implementing MTM services in your pharmacy practice.

Yet, we must remember that ideas are just the beginning. The founder of Buddhism was credited with saying "An idea that is developed and put into action is more important than an idea that exists only as an idea." Closing this book and setting it on a shelf after you've read it won't help anyone. You must commit to taking the ideas shared by your colleagues and leading change in your practice environment.

Effecting change is by no means simple and involves many steps over an extended period of time. In a 2003 article published in *Pharmacy Student*, we wrote,

"Once an opportunity for change presents itself, one must be aware of the reasons why the change is or is not already being led. The individual who seeks to lead change must be aware of the ideas and practices others have attempted to implement in similar situations. Listening to and working with others in a shared environment where the opportunity for change exists is essential. Doing this allows the creative process to thrive and the result is ideas that have been analyzed and considered from many perspectives. Ideas will be more fully developed and are more likely to be accepted by individuals who have the ability to authorize change. Then, once an idea for change has been fully explored, it is essential that we be willing to share our thoughts and desires with others. Openly communicating how change would benefit all parties involved is key to making an idea become reality. Change may not always happen exactly as it is envisioned, but following a process of learning and sharing will create a dynamic environment where the end result is positive outcomes for pharmacists and their patients."

This book is a tool that facilitates dialogue. The contributors have opened their minds to new ideas and tested them. Importantly, they have also taken time to share their experiences with you. Now it is your turn. Turn the page and browse through the ideas that span a wide range of services and strategies. Find an idea that you feel applies to your setting, run it through the rigors of consideration, and incorporate what you learn to sharpen the idea and make it your own.

Finally, create positive change in your practice environment through application of your refined strategy and come back full circle, sharing YOUR success with others.

Andrew P. Traynor, PharmD, BCPS
Todd D. Sorenson, PharmD
Center for Leading Healthcare Change
College of Pharmacy
University of Minnesota
Minneapolis, Minnesota

PREFACE

Pharmacist Ray Marcrom, an early innovator who created a thriving, cutting-edge patient care practice at his community pharmacy in Manchester, Tennessee, has said pharmacists should ask themselves, "What do we have that patients need?" instead of "Why don't patients want what we have?"

Indeed, how can we expect patients to look to us for the care-based services we can provide when 66% do not know their pharmacist's name or even have a relationship with a pharmacist? (APhA Consumer Survey, 2004).

The growth in reimbursement for care-based services, including Medication Therapy Management (MTM) services, gives each of us the opportunity to help change the public face of pharmacy. How? By showing patients, one at a time, the positive difference we, their pharmacists, can make in helping them make the best use of their medicines.

Sounds simple? It can be. Not all of us may have the immediate chance to create a comprehensive MTM service where we practice. As a pharmacist who works relief, that is true in my case. However, what I have observed through countless pharmacy shifts at countless pharmacies is that making a difference can be done every day. You just have to decide you are going to do it.

In his book, *The Fred Factor*, author Mark Sanborn describes the story of Fred Shea. Fred has a less than glamorous job of working for the U.S. Postal Service but serves his customers with exceptional service and commitment. He turns the "mundane moments of life into masterpieces."

If you can, think of what opportunities await you to help others, and in the process you can achieve deeper personal satisfaction while making a positive contribution to our profession. My friend and colleague Tracy Anderson Haag calls it the "Phred Factor."

The purpose of this book is to motivate you to change what you do by offering one hundred "easy" tips from successful practitioners who have already cleared the path toward success. The tips are short, concise, and organized by theme.

This book is not a "how to" manual for implementing MTM services or patient care. There are many resources available to help you do that. (Visit the MTM Resource Center at www. pharmacist.com.) This book is different in that it features many, many innovators. It is a practical, easy-to-use source of new ideas for practices of any size. You can pick this book up every day, once a week, or even once a month, to read about and implement a new idea.

The important thing is that you do pick this book up. No one can prevent you from being exceptional. At the end of the day, ask yourself, what kind of difference did I make?

Marsha K. Millonig

P.S. As you implement these ideas and create new ones, we'd like you to share them so we can use them in the future to share with colleagues. You can contribute your ideas at www.catalystenterprises.net.

CONTRIBUTORS

Kristin N. Ball, PharmD
Assistant Professor of Pharmacy Practice
Hampton University School of Pharmacy
Hampton, VA

Donna Bartlett, RPh
Clinical Pharmacist
MassMedLine
Massachusetts College of Pharmacy and Health Sciences
Worcester, MA

Bill Boyes, RPh
Owner, Boyes Pharmacy
Faribault, MN

Jeffrey M. Brewer, PharmD, BCPS
Clinical Pharmacy Specialist, Primary Care
The Johns Hopkins Hospital
Baltimore, MD

John M. Brislin, BPharm, CGP, FASCP
President
Pharmacist Consultation Services
Lexington, KY

Lori Brown, PharmD
Manager, Clinical Services
Kerr Drug
Raleigh, NC

Brian D. Buck, PharmD
Clinical Associate Professor
University of Georgia College of Pharmacy
Athens, GA

Anne L. Burns, BPharm
VP, Professional Affairs
APhA
Washington, DC

Landon Castleman, PharmD
Pharmacy Manager
Kroger Pharmacy
Athens, GA

Donna Cestone, RPh
Past President, New Jersey Pharmacists Association
Randolph, NJ

Rebecca W. Chater, BPharm, MPH
Director of Clinical Services
Kerr Drug
Durham, NC

Mary Choy, PharmD
Assistant Clinical Professor
St. John's University College of Pharmacy and Allied Health
Professions
Queens, NY

Donald A. Dee, BPharm, MS
Former Executive Director, Minnesota Pharmacists Association
Emily, MN and Fort Myers, FL

Paula Evans, MS
Clinical Pharmacist
MassMedLine
Massachusetts College of Pharmacy and Health Sciences
Worcester, MA

Bill G. Felkey, MS
Professor of Pharmacy Care Systems
Auburn University School of Pharmacy
Auburn University, AL

Julie Fike, PharmD, CDM
Genoa Healthcare
Anoka, MN

Heather Heitert, PharmD
Pharmacist
Kmart
Pueblo, CO

Metta Lou Henderson, BPharm, PhD
Former Associate Dean
Ohio Northern University
Raabe College of Pharmacy
Ada, OH

John Hunter, BPharm
Pharmacist
Cub Pharmacy
Bloomington, MN

Brian J. Isetts, PhD, BCPS, FAPhA
Associate Professor, Department of Pharmaceutical Care &
Health Systems
University of Minnesota College of Pharmacy
Minneapolis, MN

Brian Jensen, RPh, FACA
President
Lakeshore Apothacare, Inc.
Two Rivers, WI

Michael Koski, BPharm
IV Therapy Department Manager
PharMerica
Fridley, MN

Patty Kumbera, BPharm
COO
Outcomes Pharmaceutical Healthcare
Des Moines, IA

Angie Larson, RPh
Boyes Pharmacy
Faribault, MN

Sandra Leal, PharmD, CDE
Clinical Pharmacy Supervisor
El Rio Community Health Center
Tucson, AZ

John Loch, BPharm
Pharmacist
Cub Pharmacy
Rosemount, MN

Lucinda L. Maine, PhD
Executive Director
American Association of Colleges of Pharmacy
Alexandria, VA

Maria Maniscalco-Feichtl, BPharm, PharmD
Assistant Professor, Pharmacy Practice
Nova Southeastern University College of Pharmacy
Pharmacist, NSU Clinic Pharmacy
Fort Lauderdale, FL

Ray Marcrom, PharmD, FACA, FAPhA
President and CEO
Marcrom's Pharmacy
Manchester, TN

Thomas E. Menighan, BPharm, MBA
Syntegra, LLC
Annapolis, MD

Marsha K. Millonig, BPharm, MBA
President/CEO
Catalyst Enterprises, LLC
Eagan, MN
(651) 905-9002
mmillonig@catalystenterprises.net

Jaime Montouro, PharmD
Manager, MTM Services
SuperValu
Chicago, IL

Ruth E. Nemire, PharmD
Associate Dean for Professional Education and
Community Engagement
Touro College of Pharmacy
New York, NY

Brenna Neumann, PharmD
Director, Clinical Services
Advantage Healthcare
Neosho, MO

Allen Nichol, PharmD
Grandview Family Practice
Columbus, OH

Shay Phillips, PharmD, BCPS
Assistant Professor of Pharmacy Practice
Hampton University School of Pharmacy
Hampton, VA

Patricia Powell, PharmD
Community Pharmacy Practice Resident
Kroger Pharmacy
University of Georgia College of Pharmacy
Athens, GA

Heather Sakely, PharmD, BCPS
Pittsburgh, PA

David Schwed, BPharm, FACA
Woodruff's Drugs
Bridgeton, NJ

Steven T. Simenson, BPharm, FAPhA, FACA
President
Goodrich Pharmacies
Anoka, MN

Stan Simmons
Consumer
New York, NY

Margie Snyder, PharmD
Community Practice Research Fellow
University of Pittsburgh School of Pharmacy
Pittsburgh, PA

Melissa A. Somma McGivney, PharmD, CDE
Director
University of Pittsburgh School of Pharmacy/Rite Aid Patient
Care Initiative
Pittsburgh, PA

Judith B. Sommers Hanson, PharmD, CDM
Walgreens Health Initiative
Huntley, IL

Lori Steinemann
Pharmacy Technician
Target Pharmacy
St. Cloud, MN

Mary Sullivan, PharmD
Director, Clinical Pharmacist
MassMedLine
Massachusetts College of Pharmacy and Health Sciences
Worcester, MA

Don Thibodeau, BPharm
Clinical Pharmacist and CEO
PillHelp® Works®
Fort Myers, FL

Maya Thompson, PharmD, BCPS
Lieutenant Commander, US Public Health Service
Sells Service Unit
Chinle, AZ

Brad Tice, PharmD, PMP
PharmMD
Brentwood, TN

William N. Tindall, BPharm, PhD
Professor Emeritus
Wright State University School of Medicine
Dayton, OH

Susan Torrico, BPharm
President
AmeliaPlex, Inc.
Orlando, FL

Daniel R. Touchette, BPharm, PharmD
Assistant Professor of Pharmacoeconomics
University of Illinois at Chicago College of Pharmacy
Chicago, IL

Kari Trapskin, PharmD
Director, Health Care Quality Initiatives
Pharmacy Society of Wisconsin
Madison, WI

Yanci L. Walker, PharmD
2006-2007 Community Practice Resident
Duren Pharmacy, University of Tennessee
Knoxville, TN

David N. Zimmerman, PharmD, FASCP
Bloomfield Hills, MI

Getting Started

All glory comes from daring to begin.
Eugene F. Ware

Apply for Grants

Many organizations offer grants for both general and disease-specific patient care programs. Pharmacists can take advantage of these grants to get programs up and running. For example, the APhA Foundation provides more than 40 $1,000 grants each year through its Incentive Grants program (www.aphafoundation.org). Also, the Community Pharmacy Foundation provides resources for research and development that encourage new capabilities and continuous improvements in the delivery of patient care. They accept grant applications online at www.communitypharmacyfoundation.org.

Donna Cestone
David Schwed

☞ TIP # 2

Apply MTM Pearls from the Literature

Pharmacist Melissa Somma McGivney advises pharmacists to apply MTM pearls they read about in the literature to their practices. She now authors a monthly MTM Tip of the Month column in *Pharmacy Today* to bring the latest information on MTM advances, innovations, and opportunities to pharmacists. As pharmacists look to initiate or expand their MTM practices, experiences from others can help move the learning curve forward.

Melissa A. Somma McGivney

☞ TIP # 3

Create a Vision

Brian Jensen advises pharmacists to craft a vision for their patient care practice that focuses on drug therapy outcomes. From there, develop a work plan. His pharmacy practice uses an asset conversion model that looks at resource determination, service development, demand creation, and money management.

A pharmacy resident was instrumental in helping to create this comprehensive plan.

Brian Jensen

> *In the business world, everyone is paid in two coins: cash and experience. Take the experience first; the cash will come later.*
>
> *Harold Geneen*

 # TIP # 4

Make the Time for MTM

Bill Boyes and Angie Larson recommend that pharmacists write down their vision of an MTM practice, and then make time to conduct MTM. When determining how to incorporate MTM from a time standpoint, it is easiest to begin by scheduling MTM appointments for certain set hours and days each week. For example, with a new service, setting aside 2 to 4 hours during a pharmacist shift overlap provides the dedicated time to conduct MTM while allowing pharmacist coverage for dispensing services.

After an initial schedule is set, Bill and Angie advise training all staff about the new service and utilizing staff to help identify MTM patients and set up appointments. They also conduct patient surveys and know target patient populations. They believe seeking appropriate accreditation, such as by the American Diabetes Association (ADA) for a diabetes MTM service, is important. So is crafting advertising and marketing plans.

Bill Boyes
Angie Larson

 # TIP # 5

Just Do It

Pharmacist Heather Heitert says, "If you are interested in providing patient care services but are not sure where to start, don't be afraid to just do it." At her practice, she instituted monthly Health Topic Days to cover topics that coincide with national health observances. During the four-hour program, she hands out information, answers patient questions, and provides health screenings. The program is growing and helps patients understand the pharmacist's role beyond dispensing.

Heather Heitert

 **TIP # 6**

Keep Patients in Mind

Develop an MTM service with patients in mind. Determine how you can add value to the patient in a way that is meaningful to him or her.

Brad Tice

 **TIP # 7**

Measure Your Readiness

APhA has developed an MTM self-assessment survey that can help pharmacists gauge whether they are ready to implement MTM services. Pharmacists can use this tool to identify education and training needs and areas in the pharmacy where physical changes may be needed to accommodate MTM services.

The survey takes about 10 minutes to complete and is accessible on the pharmacist.com Web site under MTM: http://www.pharmacist.com/ AM/Template.cfm?Section=Pharmacist_ Practitioners&Template=/ TaggedPage/TaggedPageDisplay. cfm&TPLID=96&ContentID=11481.

Anne L. Burns

> *Life is a book and you are the author. You determine its plot and pace and you—only you—turn its pages.*
> *Beth Mende Conny*

 # TIP # 8

Partner with a School or College of Pharmacy

Pharmacists with an interest in building MTM services will find their local school or college of pharmacy to be an excellent partner. Many pharmacy practice faculty can help institute services, and experiential education directors will work with preceptors to develop practices.

Schools and colleges of pharmacy can also work with pharmacists to create residency programs. Additionally, you can challenge pharmacy residents to research and initiate many new patient care services.

Marsha K. Millonig

 **TIP # 9**

Start Small and Build

Pharmacist Judy Sommers Hanson advises other pharmacists to "start small" when implementing patient care programs. "Small investments can create big rewards," she says. Pharmacists do not have to create everything all at once; they can develop a program in stages. Practitioners should start in an area they feel comfortable with.

For example, if a pharmacist has an interest in blood pressure management and is good at public speaking, he could start by providing basic information sessions to patients on blood pressure. Then, he could add blood pressure screenings in the pharmacy. Once patients begin to utilize services more, Judy advises expanding these services to include MTM and disease management.

When implementing changes in your practice, gain the support of those outside the pharmacy. While working in a grocery store setting, Judy found that the more people outside the pharmacy who knew about her services, the better. For example, she had a Store Manager tell her she saved his life and a Department Manager who used her medication monitoring services to support his physician's care.

Judith B. Sommers Hanson

The innovator is not an opponent of the old; he is a proponent of the new.
Lyle E. Schaller

 # TIP # 10

Start Part-Time

Pharmacist John Brislin has created office-based pharmacy practices in Ohio and Lexington, KY, after a nearly 30-year career in hospital, long-term care, home infusion, and other pharmacy practices. He encourages pharmacists who want to build nondispensing MTM and cognitive service practices to start part-time while continuing to practice in their current position. Creating a full-time independent consulting practice from the ground up and expecting it to provide a full-time salary the first year was unrealistic—an important lesson John learned when he began his current practice. Now he has packaged his experience and markets his "lessons learned" to other motivated practitioners through the company's Consultant Practice Program.

John M. Brislin

 **TIP # 11**

Focus on Making a Difference

Tom Menighan says pharmacists he knows who have started successful MTM and patient care practices share several characteristics. They have a sense of optimism and spend their time creating options. They have good relationships, and work at meeting people and maintaining a network of both close friends and professional associates. They have a sense of control over their lives, and are deeply involved in their careers and families. They have a belief in a higher being. They have a need for lifelong learning. They have a sense of contributing to the greater good. Finally, they possess the knowledge that while looking for other things, happiness happens.

He shares the advice his first dean in pharmacy school reminded him of: you are entering a profession where you will never have to worry about making a living, so you should worry about making a difference.

Thomas E. Menighan

In many lines of work, it isn't how much you do that counts, but how much you do well and how often you decide right.
William Feather

NOTES

NOTES

2 Goal Setting and Action Plans

You seldom hit anything unless you aim at it.

Anonymous

 **TIP # 12**

Set Goals and Make Them Happen

Jeffrey Brewer and his team of caregivers in Primary Care at the Johns Hopkins Hospital believe setting goals and making them happen is a key to implementing MTM services programs. Brewer says that regardless of the practice setting or workload, if a pharmacist resolves to reach a small goal every day he will see his MTM practice grow. For example, make two drug therapy interventions per day and communicate this to colleagues, or take an extra two minutes with the sickest polypharmacy patients to ensure that their data is accurate.

Jeffrey M. Brewer

*Only those who dare to fail greatly
can ever achieve greatly.*

Robert F. Kennedy

 **TIP # 13**

Join a Pilot Project

Pharmacists have a great opportunity to implement MTM services by joining pilot initiatives. The Wisconsin Pharmacy Quality Collaborative (WPQC) is a good example. Established July 17, 2006, the WPQC is dedicated to aligning incentives for both pharmacists and payers, creating a uniform set of pharmacist-provided medication management services, and developing a quality credentialing process in Wisconsin through a collaborative venture between third-party payers (health plans, employers and government agencies) and pharmacy providers in the state. The expected results of this health care quality initiative include:

1. Improved medication use among enrolled patients as evidenced by attaining specific patient care outcomes.

2. Improved patient safety, including decreased numbers of medication errors and adverse drug events.

3. Reduced health care costs for participating payers.

4. Professional recognition and compensation based upon the development and implementation of pharmacy practice services that improve the use and safety of medications.

To be included in the pilot network, pharmacies must possess a required set of services and characteristics. WPQC endorses these requirements as "best practices" that maximize patient safety in the medication use process.

Kari Trapskin

 **TIP # 14**

Implement Continuous Quality Improvement Measures

Each patient encounter, billing process, and follow-up visit provides an opportunity to learn about and improve a pharmacist's MTM services. Use quality measures, checkpoints, and mechanisms to continuously adapt and improve your MTM practice.

Melissa A. Somma McGivney

NOTES

Identifying, Monitoring, and Educating Patients

Recruit Patients

Kristin Ball encourages pharmacists to avoid mailing out hundreds of brochures to advertise their services. Citing an abstract presented at a national pharmacy meeting, she states that mass mailing is the most ineffective method for recruiting patients for a community-based disease state management program. Unfortunately, she also became aware of this fact through experience. After implementing a diabetes management program in an independent pharmacy, Kristin was ready to start recruiting patients. She typed an inform-ative yet concise letter, and mailed it to all the patients who had received a diabetes drug in the prior four months. She included a full-color tri-fold brochure on the program. She thought she would hear back from so many people that she would have to turn some away. Unfortunately, that was not the case. Her efforts resulted in inquiries from three patients. She could not believe the slow response.

In-store recruiting included a full-color 24" x 36" sign displayed in the pharmacy and the brochures. "Brochures are great to keep in the store for distribution to patients who are interested," notes Kristin. When developing brochures, she reminds pharmacists to keep in mind the reading level of the target audience. Kristin has found that the most effective method of recruiting patients was to simply approach them when they visited the pharmacy to pick up or drop off prescriptions. She can almost guarantee recruitment with this approach. After three weeks of using this method, she had recruited about 12 patients— without cost to her or the pharmacy owner.

Kristin N. Ball

> *When you shoot for the moon and you come up short, you still end up among the stars.*
>
> *Les Brown*

TIP # 16

Work from Prescription Drug Plan Lists

Steve Simenson of Goodrich Pharmacies notes that it's relatively easy for pharmacists to identify their dispensing customers who have multiple chronic illnesses and are eligible for reimbursable MTM. Accessing the countless other eligibles in an area, however, can be difficult. "There are literally a thousand MTM eligibles next door, but because they go to someone else for order fulfillment, they are not sent to us for MTM," says Steve. He recommends that community pharmacists contact prescription drug plans and let them know they offer MTM services. Plans offering pharmacist-delivered MTM can give pharmacists a list of their eligible beneficiaries.

Steven T. Simenson

TIP # 17

Use Pharmacy Technicians

You can actively involve technicians in identifying potential candidates for MTM and managing physician referrals. For example, give technicians a checklist of criteria for identifying potential candidates for MTM while working at the dispensing counter (e.g., patient takes multiple medications, patient being treated for one or more chronic diseases). Technicians can also set up charts for new patients and send thank-you letters to physicians who refer patients to the practice.

Margie Snyder

TIP # 18

Participate in Pharmacy-Based Research Networks

Some national and state organizations have created Pharmacy-Based Research Networks that utilize pharmacy practice sites to conduct Phase IV post-marketing surveillance and other practice research, such as rates of immunization or MTM service trends. This research often carries reimbursement and is a natural extension of MTM services.

Marsha K. Millonig

 # TIP # 19

Prepare for Visits and Keep Them on Time

Yanci Walker was fortunate to participate in the forefront of MTM services in a community pharmacy setting. As a resident, Yanci was given a unique gift that not many practicing community pharmacists are given—time. Scheduling, conducting, and documenting an MTM session can be extremely rewarding, but also quite costly with regard to a pharmacist's time. The key in balancing the two is preparation. If possible, delegate the scheduling to a nonpharmacist employee.

Yanci and colleagues recognized that if a service is provided free, patients might not see value in it. Therefore, they set out to show patients the value of an MTM session by presenting it as a cost-saving and educational opportunity. They documented some examples of how the MTM service saved money for patients. By doing so, the practitioners were able to convince patients to schedule an appointment for the new service. They experienced many missed appointments, so they began providing reminder calls that made a world of difference.

When you prepare for an appointment, review the patient's medication profile and preprint any needed documents. Refer to clinical guidelines based on the patient's presenting disease states. Before the patient arrives, compile a list of questions and key points to discuss during the appointment to keep sessions on track and on time.

Yanci also recommends that pharmacists use patient counseling handouts and educational literature. In the practice, they document appointments using a SOAP note format in a commercial software package, and bill for services.

Yanci reflects, "Although I have just begun my career, I recognize that 'bill for your services' is a concept which experienced pharmacists have both fought for and anticipated implementing for many years. MTM is the first step in actualizing this concept and demonstrating the value of pharmaceutical care."

Yanci L. Walker

You may occasionally give out,
but never give up.

Mary Crowley

 # TIP # 20

Tailor Patient Visits

When Kristin Ball first began to offer diabetes management education as a community pharmacy practice resident, she would provide foot screenings; measure A1C, blood pressure, cholesterol and glucose; and educate patients on meal planning, self-monitoring of blood glucose techniques, physical activity, sick day management, and any other issues she could squeeze in before the patient got restless! During follow-up calls to see how things were going, she found many patients could not remember all the information she had provided during the initial visit. After the first three patients, she realized she was doing too much too fast. So she began focusing on one area of diabetes management per 30 to 45 minute visit with each patient. She found the patients retained the information a lot better and did not mind spending 30 minutes with her each month when they picked up their medication.

Kristin N. Ball

What the mind can conceive and believe, it can achieve.

Napoleon Hill

 # TIP # 21

Send Multiple Patient Reminders

When a new patient agrees to MTM, Steve Simenson sends him or her a confirmation reminder. "Patients make the appointment but easily forget it. It's not that high on their priority list, so on the day before the appointment, we call to make sure they know where to come, the time, what we're going to do, and what they can bring." He also notes that it helps to remind patients to bring a printout of all their medications.

Steven T. Simenson

☞ TIP # 22

Obtain Laboratory Data

An integral part of MTM services is evaluating patient-specific laboratory monitoring data. However, obtaining such data can be a challenge. For starters, pharmacists need to establish working relationships with physicians and their office staff. Patients should also be encouraged to "know their numbers" and obtain laboratory information from their physicians. Pharmacists can request this data as well. Finally, pharmacists should consider establishing point-of-care (POC) testing in the practice and providing this information to both the patient and his or her physician.

Melissa A. Somma McGivney

☞ TIP # 23

Plan for the Next Visit

The documentation that a pharmacist creates from a patient encounter serves as the map or plan for the next MTM visit. Planning the next visit at the end of the current visit is an efficient and effective way to allow the pharmacist to pick up where he or she left off, so he or she or one of his or her colleagues can proceed with the visit. Share the plan with the patient so that he or she knows what to expect at the next visit.

Melissa A. Somma McGivney

The greatest achievements are those that benefit others.
Lillian Gilchrest

☞ TIP # 24

Provide a Medication Reminder Service for High-Risk Noncompliant Patients

Susan Torrico recommends pharmacists provide a medication reminder service for high-risk, noncompliant patients. She notes that by utilizing an online Internet alert service for scheduling and delivering reminders, pharmacists can effectively improve compliance rates and increase refills in the process. One system that she has created provides automated alerts via cell phone, land line, alphanumeric pagers, and email systems on PCs or wireless devices. "Providing patients with automated reminders to take their medications on a routine schedule is, by definition, medication management of the highest order," says Susan. The majority of patients—70% to 80%—who admit that they often miss doses are in the 45-to-60 year age range. They forget doses because they get busy and distracted, and reminders can be a welcome solution. For high-risk patients such as organ transplant recipients, people with diabetes, AIDS or heart disease, reminders can be a lifesaver.

Susan Torrico

☞ TIP # 25

Upgrade Glucose Meters

Pharmacist Julie Fike recommends that pharmacists ask patients with prescriptions for older test strips how old their glucose meters are. This is an easy way to open a discussion about newer meters that have improved features. For example, some machines have the strips contained inside the machine. This can be easier for patients with arthritis. These machines are also "code-free," so the patient does not have to match a code on the bottle of strips. Taking away this extra step can reduce the percentage of error by up to 43%. She notes that meter manufacturer sales representatives may offer free vouchers that can be helpful in convincing patients to "upgrade" to new machines.

Once a patient picks a new machine, Julie contacts the doctor using a form she created to obtain required information, including prescriptions for the machine, test strips, lancets, and control solution. She asks the doctor to "fill in the blank" for the times per day to test, asks for one year of refills, and also has the doctor circle either "insulin dependent" or "non-insulin dependent" to make claims processing much easier. Forms are signed and faxed back to the pharmacy, fulfilling all Medicare requirements. She says the form has helped reduce the prescription turnaround time to about one day.

Once she receives the prescription, Julie calls the patient and sets up an appointment for meter teaching. During the appointment, she demonstrates the machine and has the patient demonstrate it back to her to ensure understanding. She sets the time of day on the machine and makes sure the patient fills out the warranty card. She also gives the patient an easy 1-2-3 picture-based testing sheet (also available from the meter manufacturer sales representative) to help him or her once he returns home.

Patients are encouraged to visit the pharmacy if they need additional help. "Doing this demonstrates the value of the community pharmacist, because meter teaching is not something a patient can get from a mail order pharmacy," says Julie.

Julie Fike

 **TIP # 26**

Use Free Resources

Pharmacist Donna Cestone has spent much of her career within the pharmaceutical industry. She and her New Jersey colleague David Schwed recommend pharmacists take advantage of free patient-oriented resources that industry firms often make available either on web sites or through their sales representatives. Examples include disease-specific brochures, testing log books for blood pressure and blood glucose, and diet and exercise guidelines, among others.

Donna Cestone
David Schwed

*You must give your own story
to the world.*

Carter C. Woodsen

 **TIP # 27**

Use Motivational Interviewing

Motivational interviewing is one way that pharmacy staff can "work smarter, not harder" in their delivery of MTM services. Motivational interviewing is designed to allow pharmacists to engage their patients in discussions that inform patients and allow them to be more involved in their own self-care. It involves eliciting information from the patient, providing feedback, then ensuring patient understanding.

For example, say that one of your patients is taking his or her blood pressure medicine every other day rather than every day in an effort to stretch co-pays and make the medication more affordable. You can elicit this information when the patient comes in for a refill that is late. Using motivational interviewing techniques, you would empathize with the patient's need to save money, but then try to provide information about the risks associated with not taking the blood pressure medication, including a possible stroke or heart attack. Because the patient does not want to suffer these negative health consequences, he or she may be motivated to take the medication correctly. To address co-pay issues you might be able to offer an alternative medication or provide prescription drug assistance resources.

Maya Thompson

 # TIP # 28

Seek Simplicity and Ask the Right Questions

Mike Koski shares a case where a 70-year-old white female patient with an infected total knee arthroplasty was being managed on IV Vancomycin 1gm every 24 hours. The patient had three laboratory draws to determine Vancomycin blood levels; all were therapeutic. On the fourth laboratory draw, however, the level was reported as low. The pharmacist contacted the nursing facility to confirm that the patient was receiving the dose. The nurse reviewed the medication administration record, and noted that the dose had been initialed as given each day. The pharmacist asked to speak with the nurse administering the medication.

The pharmacist discovered that the nurse was not familiar with the drug infusion system that was being used, and was only infusing saline because she failed to properly activate the system to mix the drug with the saline. This was a case where the pharmacist needed to look for the simplest answer, but had to ask the proper questions.

Michael Koski

Somewhere, someone is looking for exactly what you have to offer.
Louise L. Hay

NOTES

4 Physician/Pharmacist Collaborative Relationships

TIP # 29

Avoid Jargon

When dealing with people in another profession, avoid using technical jargon that can hinder your ability to reach a common understanding of what is being said. Many physicians may not know what MTM means. Pharmacists should be prepared to educate them.

William N. Tindall

TIP # 30

Build Physician Relationships

Being the only clinical pharmacist providing pharmaceutical care services in a physician-dominated practice can be daunting. This is what Shay Phillips faced when she became an assistant professor tasked with starting clinical services in an outpatient teaching institution that offered more than 18 different specialty clinics. Although Shay welcomed the challenge, she felt overwhelmed. Walking into the facility the first day, she had no idea where to start, but she had lots of questions that needed answering quickly. They included:

- What pharmacy service does this facility need most?
- What is the best way to prove my worth?
- How do we cultivate positive pharmacist–physician relationships?
- How do we make physicians comfortable enough with our clinical skills to provide referrals with confidence?
- How do we make sure our pharmacotherapy knowledge is always one step above theirs?

With these questions in mind, Shay mapped out a tentative plan of attack and then proceeded cautiously and with diplomacy. She knew that whatever practices were currently conducted, she would need to accomplish much more to prove her worth.

For the first couple of days, Shay observed how the clinic operated:

- What procedures were the employees currently using to update medication lists?
- How did they deal with noncompliance?
- How comprehensive was pharmacological and nonpharmacological education?
- Were medications being used according to guidelines?

Shay began rounding with the attending and resident physicians in the various clinics. Being exposed to all the clinics helped her determine her strengths and weaknesses in disease state management. For the first few days, she did not make any recommendations. Rather, she listened intently to other clinicians' patient treatment discussions, information references, and prescribing patterns.

The first challenge Shay encountered was getting physicians used to her presence. She advises other pharmacists not to underestimate how dependability and presence helps form working relationships. She also recommends finding out how you can make the relationship work for all parties involved.

When you are new to a situation and practitioners are not comfortable with pharmacists' clinical knowledge, Shay notes that you have to demonstrate your worth slowly. Being too aggressive too soon may not be the best approach to take. If you're good, you will accomplish what you set out to do, but patience and timing are important.

Shay also attended several dinners hosted by pharmaceutical companies that clinic physicians attended. This allowed relationship building in a more relaxed environment. While onsite, Shay kept cultivating the relationships through daily rounding and making evidence-based therapy recommendations. After each patient diagnosis, Shay would confidently voice her recommendations. Soon her fellow health care colleagues were asking for her clinical judgment.

Shay Phillips

You have to think anyway,
so why not think big?

Donald Trump

 TIP # 31

Conduct Physician In-Services

Offer to conduct some in-service drug therapy training programs for a medical practice. If pharmaceutical representatives can do it, why not you?

William N. Tindall

TIP # 32

Create a Postcard for Physicians

One pharmacist built his relationship and trust with a physician by preprinting post cards that simply stated, "Today I refilled your prescription for _____ for your patient _____. She/he is taking the refilled medication as per your instructions."

William N. Tindall

 **TIP # 33**

Inform Physicians about Your MTM Service

Informing area physicians about your MTM practice can be a good way to build referrals. Bill advises setting up an appointment in advance and carefully preparing to keep things efficient during the visit. Pharmacists should clearly state why they are visiting and the time they will spend. Deliver information without bluster and embellishment, get to the point, and be factual. Focus on information vital to better patient care, rather than information that is "nice to know." Close the call by asking the physician what you can do to be a resource for the practice and its patients.

William N. Tindall

People's behavior makes sense if you think about it in terms of their goals, needs, and motives.

Thomas Mann

 **TIP # 34**

Develop a Physician Newsletter

Pharmacists should consider developing a newsletter and distributing it to physicians in their area. Make sure to include physicians whose prescriptions are not filled at your pharmacy. Consider featuring a patient's story that includes how the MTM program contributed to the patient's quality of life. Physicians like patient stories, and appreciate knowing there is a "safety net" of interdisciplinary expertise that they can call upon.

William N. Tindall

 **TIP # 35**

Focus on the Patient

Whenever you talk to a physician, always position his or her patient as the beneficiary of any MTM intervention. Explain how this benefit resulted from all parties working together on a common patient care goal.

William N. Tindall

Learn about the Physician's Practice

Kristin Ball began a diabetes management program in an independent pharmacy while serving as a community pharmacy practice resident. Before she began to recruit patients, she visited local physician offices and gave 15-minute presentations on the services she would offer and how she could assist them with managing their patients with diabetes. One of the physicians as well as most of his patients were Hispanic. Although he was excited about working with Kristin, he had a major concern about her inability to speak Spanish in order to effectively communicate with his patients. She immediately sensed his apprehension about referring his patients to her.

Fortunately, there were two Hispanic pharmacy technicians at the pharmacy where she was completing her residency. She asked the pharmacy owners if they would compensate a technician to work with her to provide translation skills. They agreed, and one week after her initial meeting with the physician, she was able to inform him that the communication barrier issue was resolved.

Kristin advises others to be mindful of the interests/needs of the practitioner, especially when you want to work with a practitioner whose patients are unique in any way.

Kristin N. Ball

 # TIP # 37

Build Collaborations with Physicians

Pharmacist Bill Tindall offers these strategies for developing successful collaborative relationships between pharmacists and physicians:

- Develop joint statements that support the rights of patients to be involved in making informed decisions in matters affecting drug therapy. State why the patient's trust, safety, and relationship with caregivers always come first.

- Host jointly sponsored professional meetings, especially at the local level, to help develop widespread understanding and awareness of physician and pharmacist responsibilities in drug therapy and why a collaborative approach to drug therapy benefits all.
- Build an acceptable communication, administrative, and documentation system that allows pharmacists to share relevant patient information in accordance with applicable ethical standards, accepted medical and pharmacy practice, and state and federal statutes and regulations to allow continuity of care.
- Collaborate on technology developments to enhance communication in practices (e.g., shared patient databases relevant to drug therapy).

William N. Tindall

Success is empty if you arrive at the finish line alone. The best reward is to get there surrounded by winners. The more winners you can bring with you, the more gratifying the victory.
Howard Schultz

 **TIP # 38**

Tell Physicians When You Support Their Patient's Care

Collaboration between health professionals, especially physicians and pharmacists, can generate better drug therapy outcomes. The cornerstone of what makes this work is trust and confidence in each other, says pharmacist Bill Tindall.

In his work at the Wright State University School of Medicine, Bill has created collaborative practices between pharmacists and physicians. He advises taking great care when calling physician offices or answering the pharmacy phone. Make sure you say your name and identify yourself as a pharmacist.

Bill observes that physicians know healing is a multifactorial event, but they often do not perceive pharmacists as part of that event. He advises pharmacists to let the physician know whenever they take actions to support care of the physician's patients by calling, faxing, and/or giving patients information which they can share during their next appointment with the physician.

William N. Tindall

☞ TIP # 39

Use a Checklist of What Works

Brock and Doucette (*J Am Pharm Assoc.* 2004; 44:358-365) outline six variables that differentiate early-stage and late-stage collaboration between physicians and pharmacists. These variables are:

- Development of bidirectional communication.
- Caring for mutual patients.
- Identification of win-win opportunities.
- Adding value to the medical practice.
- Physician convenience.
- Movement toward a balanced dependence between the pharmacist and physician.

Pharmacists should use this as a checklist and ask physicians how well they are doing in regard to building their relationships.

William N. Tindall

 **TIP # 40**

Use Scripts and Role-Playing

Communication between pharmacists can be a barrier to implementing MTM services. At his institution, Jeffrey Brewer's team is working from a standardized patient presentation script to ensure a common communication approach by every pharmacist on the team.

The pharmacist–physician relationship is different for each pharmacy because of geography, patient population, and the provider's practice location. To address this, they may use scripts and role playing to facilitate interprofessional dialogue between the pharmacist at the pharmacy and local physicians—a sort of "trial run" for communicating with other health professionals. Once pharmacists have seen several patients under a physician's care, they are able to solidify the pharmacist–physician relationship based on their knowledge base.

Jeffrey M. Brewer

NOTES

 # TIP # 41

Coordinate Multiple Systems

Documenting MTM services can be an issue because there is no industry standardization. At Jeffrey Brewer's institution, they start with paper databases and utilize the insurance-specific billing systems to gain reimbursement. He believes the optimal documentation system would integrate with the dispensing system, allowing both clinical and operational data to be processed and reported. Until such systems are developed, pharmacists will need to balance multiple systems to make this service-based model work.

Jeffrey M. Brewer

☞ TIP # 42

Know the Documentation Components

Jay Currie and colleagues describe the key components of pharmacist-provided patient care documentation in *J Am Pharm Assoc.* 2003; 43:41-49. They include the visit description, patient history, and pharmacist assessment/plan. You can view these resources at www.pharmacist.com under MTM.

Melissa A. Somma McGivney

☞ TIP # 43

Get Administrative Work Done Before the Visit

Before an MTM client comes into the pharmacy, Steve Simenson's staff gets all the secretarial work done. This includes gathering any information about the client—such as name, address, phone number, prescriptions, and supplements—and entering the requisite documentation into a database.

Steven T. Simenson

 **TIP # 44**

Keep It Simple and Keep Simplifying

In her many years implementing pharmaceutical care and MTM services programs, Patty Kumbera has found it helpful to keep documentation simple and to find ways to keep simplifying it. For example, she uses color-coded patient education and monitoring forms to help visually track issue identification, actions taken, and outcomes. She also automates encounters, and recommends that pharmacists quantify the value of their services.

To help quantify the value of service, Outcomes Pharmaceutical Healthcare uses an "Estimated Cost Avoidance" model. "Pharmacists need to think about delivering value to both the patient and payer right at the start of implementing their program," Patty notes. Using a stand-ardized model can simplify documenting value.

Patty Kumbera

 **TIP # 45**

Use an OTC SOAP Note Form

Pharmacist innovator Ray Marcrom suggests practitioners use an OTC SOAP note form to create value in the mind of patients when you provide an OTC consultation. Marcrom has created a "Post-It-Note" size form that he uses for every OTC consult. He makes quick notes for the patient on the form, using the subjective, objective, assessment, plan (SOAP) format and gives it to the patient to take home. Having a tangible piece of paper with recommendations can serve as a powerful reminder to patients of their pharmacist's value.

Ray Marcrom

Success means we go to sleep at night knowing that our talents and abilities were used in a way that served others.
Marianne Williamson

NOTES

NOTES

TIP # 46

Ask for Payment

Pharmacist Don Thibodeau retreated to the Maine woods twelve years ago to reflect on his pharmacy career. He was frustrated that he could not provide as much care to patients as he wanted in the busy dispensing pharmacy where he practiced. He made a list of the skills he was most proud of, including his ability to communicate, hoping he could find a way to change his career.

Don chose to pursue an office-based pharmacy practice and designed a practice protocol. He began charging for medication management, education, and patient advocacy. As Don reflects, "They hired me. They paid me. They expressed gratitude." Twelve years later, they still do. Don also shares his experiences through an MTM Office Suite of software called PillHelp® Works®.

Don Thibodeau

 **TIP # 47**

Individualize Billing

Billing for MTM visits is as individualized as each payer contract. Some payers accept claims via the dispensing system, web-based documentation systems, and a universal claim form (CMS-1500), among others. Determining the appropriate billing method for each payer can take time. Creating a "superbill" as physician offices do can save time during the visit. Leigh Ann Baker provides an example in the September 2006 *Family Practice Management* (www.aafp.org/fpm/20060900/43inse.html.)

Melissa A. Somma McGivney

TIP # 48

Join Performance-Based Networks

Allen Nichol notes from his experience with Ohio Department of Health's Bureau for Children with Medical Handicaps that pharmacists providing MTM services need to network to offer services, rather than compete for the MTM business. A performance-based network can serve pharmacists in negotiating MTM service contracts. Allen points to the Iowa Center for Pharmaceutical Care and its relationship with Outcomes Pharmaceutical Healthcare.

A number of other communities in the United States participate in MTM service programs, and many are offered through various APhA Foundation programs. Visiting the Foundation's web site at www.aphafoundation.org may provide a helpful source of information for those seeking networks.

Allen Nichol

 **TIP # 49**

Position Programs for Payment

Several years ago when he owned his own pharmacy, John Loch realized that he had many patients with diabetes who needed more information concerning their medical condition. Many had never had any education about diabetes; others had attended a two-hour course provided by their clinic and paid for by their insurance company. So he decided to start a support group for patients with diabetes. He purchased a number of resources, including a "how-to manual" from the American Diabetes Association. He advertised in the newspaper, informed local physicians and the few diabetes educators in the area, and placed notices on prescriptions of his patients with diabetes.

John ran the group for 3 years. As many as 30 to 40 patients and family members attended the meetings, and soon people were calling him from a radius of 10 to 15 miles. He expanded the pharmacy's diabetes supplies, invited other health professionals and sales representatives to give presentations at meetings, and quickly earned the reputation of being knowledgeable about diabetes medications. This led to requests from other support groups. Although he didn't charge for these lessons, there was a donation jar on the table that raised $10 to $20 dollars per session.

Looking back, John believes he could have charged a per-session fee or fee for the entire course, especially if he had positioned it as diabetes education rather than a support group. After he reluctantly disbanded the group, he did charge a patient and his spouse $200 for 10 one-hour personalized sessions. They paid out-of-pocket.

John Loch

There are many wonderful things that will never be done if you do not do them.
Charles D. Gill

 # TIP # 50

Track MTM and Cognitive Service Payments

Tracking cash flow affiliated with MTM and other cognitive services for both pilot and permanent programs can be challenging. Unlike traditional pharmacy business model sales and profits that are tracked through POS and dispensing systems, many MTM services are administered through online databases. Complicating billing and payment tracking further are services offered across multiple sites under common ownership.

To solve this problem at Advantage Healthcare's two community and one licensed consulting pharmacies, Brenna created identical "charge accounts" for every patient care program in each location's POS system (e.g., Community Care Rx MTM encounters, Missouri Medicaid Disease State Management services, Asthma Intervention Program). When a claim for service is billed online, a pharmacy technician or the pharmacist responsible for the encounter posts the specific charge into the POS system using the register's keys for that account. Payment cycles for these programs vary from two weeks to several months, Brenna notes. The company's accountant and third-party specialist post the payment to the specific "charge account" when it is received. Billing and payment reconciliation information can then be viewed through POS system reports. Brenna notes that, using this method, payments accompanied by an "Explanation of Benefits" are easier to correctly post to each store.

Brenna Neumann

 **TIP # 51**

Use CPT Codes

Pharmacist Allen Nichol participates in the Ohio Department of Health's (ODH) MTM program. The program is offered through the ODH's Bureau for Children with Medical Handicaps (BCMH), and targets children with asthma and diabetes. MTM services are provided through a credentialed pharmacist network. Allen notes BCMH adopted the American Medical Association's Current Procedural and Terminology (CPT) codes to document and pay for these services.

First adopted in 2005 and categorized as "emerging procedures and services," CPT codes for pharmacist-provided MTM services are now officially a permanent part of the most widely used health care classification system. The AMA CPT Editorial Panel met in February 2007 and decided to upgrade the codes for providing individual, face-to-face patient assessments and medication therapy-related interventions from temporary Category III to permanent Category I status. They based this decision on evidence that pharmacists provide MTM services nationwide to hundreds of thousands of patients and that the temporary codes were widely used. The Pharmacist Services Technical Advisory Coalition (PSTAC) presented survey data to the CPT Editorial Panel showing that a total of 2.8 million face-to-face MTM encounters were conducted between 2004 and 2006. In nongovernmental settings, 86% of the encounters were in ambulatory care practices such as clinics and community pharmacies. The full survey results were published in the July/August 2007 *Journal of the American Pharmacists Association (J Am Pharm Assoc.* 2007; 47: 491-495).

The new CPT codes took effect January 1, 2008. Briefly, the codes are as follows:

- 99605—MTM service(s) provided by a pharmacist to an individual patient during a face-to-face encounter that involves an assessment and intervention (if provided); used to code the initial 15 minutes of an initial encounter with a new MTM patient.
- 99606—Initial 15 minutes with an established patient.

- 99607—Each additional 15 minutes of an initial or subsequent MTM encounter; listed separately in addition to code for primary service and in conjunction with 99605 or 99606.

The MTM codes were developed collaboratively by members of the PSTAC, comprising representatives from APhA, the American College of Clinical Pharmacy, the Academy of Managed Care Pharmacy, the American Society of Consultant Pharmacists, the American Society of Health-System Pharmacists, the National Association of Chain Drug Stores, and the National Community Pharmacists Association.

Allen Nichol

When you start doing what you really love to do, you'll never work another day in your life.

Brian Tracy

NOTES

TIP # 52

Research Technologies that Support MTM Services

If you are considering the addition of MTM services into a traditional pharmacy practice, you should be encouraged to know that literally hundreds of technologies exist to do a significant amount of the work for you. Most of this technology is readily available and very affordable.

How this technology will integrate into a practice's workflow largely depends on the pharmacy management system vendor's development in this area. For example, some pharmacy management systems already contain clinical patient record-keeping fields. Other companies produce a pharmaceutical care product and then later add distribution capabilities to their system.

The good news is that your ability to work through the entire clinical process (from appraisal to intervention to evaluation to monitoring and follow-up) are covered by an impressive array of stand-alone workstation and web-based products. All of the therapeutic outcome monitoring technologies and many of the multimedia resources to educate patients, improve their medication adherence, and provide them with customized language options are readily available. For example, if you want to specialize in addressing medication adherence problems, there are over 160 products that will help people remember to take their medicine, remember if they've taken their medicine, reduce their regimen complexity, and even help them get their refills on chronic medications.

Bill Felkey makes a great offer to colleagues. Do your research by using Internet search engines such as Google, contact your pharmacy system vendor to see what products have been integrated into your base system, and conduct some site visits where colleagues are actively providing MTM services. When you have completed these steps, you have Bill's permission to contact him by telephone (334-844-8360) or e-mail (felkebg@auburn.edu) and he will attempt to match you with the best technology to meet your needs. Bill's total work focus is to evaluate health care technology and attempt to pre-certify and pre-select those products that are capable of making you more efficient and effective.

Bill G. Felkey

 TIP # 53

Establish Personal Medication Records for Patients

Pharmacist Rebecca Chater recommends that pharmacists establish personal medication records for each patient and schedule an annual comprehensive medication review— core elements of an MTM program. The records should list OTC drugs and dietary supplements, as well as prescription medications.

Rebecca W. Chater

 **TIP # 54**

Use a PDA

As a relief pharmacist, I can't always be certain if my favorite drug references will be at the pharmacy where I'll be practicing. As a result, I rely on my own resources by carrying a personal digital assistant (PDA) with several drug information databases, clinical guidelines, and calculation programs. I'm always up to date because I "hot sync" the PDA before every shift I practice.

Marsha K. Millonig

The future belongs to those who see possibilities before they become obvious.

John Sculley

Workflow and Staffing

☞ TIP # 55

Create a Separate MTM Area

Make sure your MTM occurs in a separate, private consultation area. Stock that area with key items such as an A1C machine, blood pressure unit, a cholestech unit, and a computerized documentation system. Build the space so that it is clearly different from the dispensing area. "Presentation is really important," says Steve Simenson. "If it doesn't look like a different process, patients aren't going to realize it's a different process. Don't try to do it from behind or beside the counter. Seated, face-to-face encounters with a pharmacist MTM provider at the initial visit are the most productive."

Steven T. Simenson

☞ TIP # 56

Create a Patient Care Management Team

Comprehensive patient care requires team-work. Pharmacists should consider creating a patient care management team responsible for designing, evaluating, and expanding the MTM program. Also, get input from everyone who will be involved with an MTM practice.

Melissa A. Somma McGivney

☞ TIP # 57

Create Specialized Technician Roles

While preparing for a Pharmacy 101 lecture on "The Role of the Pharmacy Technician" at the University of Missouri–Kansas City School of Pharmacy, Brenna Neumann found an excellent article entitled, "Data Analyst Technician: An Innovative Role for the Pharmacy Technician" in the *American Journal of Health-System Pharmacy (Am J Health-Syst Pharm.* 2001;58:

1815-8). Following the principles set forth in the article, she created a Clinical Assistant Technician position in her community pharmacy setting. The Clinical Assistant Technician spends 4 to 8 hours each week assisting pharmacists with administrative tasks associated with MTM service programs, including patient scheduling and service billing. For example, the technician calls patients to make new appointments and/or to remind them of existing appointments. The technician also sends monthly news items to the Diabetes Support Group. It has been a welcome addition to the Advantage Healthcare staffing structure.

Brenna Neumann

*Surround yourself with people
who believe you can.*

Dan Zadra

☞ TIP # 58

Assign Responsibilities

Steve Simenson recommends assigning pharmacy students or assistants to handle minutiae, marketing, calling, data entry, and nonexpert MTM responsibilities. "You can't be afraid to differentiate roles," says Steve. "And the pharmacist is the most expensive cog in the wheel." The pharmacist can then focus on interviewing and assessment. "If you think the pharmacist should do everything from A to Z, it will never work. You have to keep your costs down. It's just like a medical or dental office: The dentist or physician doesn't do everything. You've got to optimize where you can."

Steven T. Simenson

 **TIP # 59**

Solicit Help from Pharmacy Technicians

As a new community pharmacy resident, Kristin Ball wanted to establish a diabetes self-management program. However, trying something new in a well-established environment is challenging and definitely requires the cooperation of co-workers. In Kristin's case, the pharmacy technicians already felt overworked. Yet, she knew she would need their help with recruiting patients into the program.

After talking to the pharmacy owners, Kristin planned a staff meeting for all ten pharmacy employees to educate them about the new service. They met before the store opened, with orange juice and pastries. Kristin gave a 20-minute presentation on the program. She focused on why a diabetes self-management program was important and how each staffer could play a role in helping people maintain healthier lives. She asked each person a question at the end of the presentation, making sure he or she understood the information presented. Whenever someone answered correctly, he or she received a gift card to a local retailer. By the meeting's end, everyone had earned a gift card, and each realized the part they could play in helping inform patients about the program. Kristin also told them that there would be a reward for the technician who recruited the most patients.

After seeing her face-to-face approach to recruiting patients, the pharmacy staff became more comfortable with the idea. She was really surprised to hear staffers tell patients about the program, even when they thought she was not paying attention.

Kristin N. Ball

Just because you can't do everything doesn't mean you shouldn't do something.

Earl Nightengale

TIP # 60

Make Patients Comfortable

What circumstances make you as a patient feel comfortable asking questions, seeking advice, or placing trust in a health care practitioner? How can these ideas be applied in your practice to create a welcoming atmosphere for your patients? Consider creating an educational resource center in the pharmacy as well as implementing health awareness campaigns in conjunction with national health observances. Visit www.healthfinder.gov/library/nho for listings.

Melissa A. Somma McGivney

TIP # 61

Schedule MTM Services

Pharmacists should consider designating one day a week to provide MTM services during pharmacist shift overlaps. This can effectively address the time factors that may be a barrier to MTM.

Lori Brown
Jaime Montouro

 **TIP # 62**

Set MTM Times and Consider Subcontracting

Many pharmacy practices find it difficult to get an MTM program going and maintain momentum. To overcome this, Brian Isetts advises pharmacists that it is important to set the hours and days when you will provide MTM services.

Some practices find it difficult to use existing staff to provide MTM services. Brian suggests that pharmacists consider subcontracting these services to bright, energetic, perhaps new pharmacists who can come into the practice and take care of patients on certain days of the week (e.g., Tuesdays and Thursdays from 9:00 a.m. - 3:00 p.m.).

Brian notes that pharmacists who are able to get a practice site to a 6-month implementation milepost find that they gain enough momentum to carry the program through to success.

Brian J. Isetts

Support Systems

Attend MTM Meetings

Many meetings feature MTM sessions, including annual MTM conferences. These meetings provide excellent avenues to gain tips and find practitioners who have paved the way before you. Set a goal to attend at least one new meeting a year. For every meeting you attend, become acquainted with one new colleague.

Marsha K. Millonig

In times of change, learners inherit the earth, while the learned find themselves beautifully equipped to deal with a world that no longer exists.
Eric Hoffer

☞ TIP # 64

Network with Colleagues

Networking with other pharmacists is a great way to learn new ideas and keep current. Judy Sommers Hanson finds preparing herself through training programs or professional meetings motivates her and serves as a way to build her network. The APhA Annual Meeting is her professional recharge.

Judy hopes pharmacists do not become intimidated to network with their peers both at meetings and after they return home. She says her greatest successes have come from input she's received from peers.

Judith B. Sommers Hanson

☞ TIP # 65

Network and Mentor

Former Ohio Northern University Pharmacy School Associate Dean Metta Lou Henderson advises a heavy regimen of networking and mentoring to students and pharmacists. Student pharmacists should join organizations at the college level. Then, get involved. She says, "You don't have to be the president, but at least do committee work and attend the meetings. Then go to a regional and/or national meeting. Use the organization to meet others. For example, fraternities are very helpful in meeting alums."

For young pharmacists, she recommends introducing yourself to someone older. Then follow him or her around at a meeting. He or she will then introduce you to others. Older pharmacists should introduce themselves to younger pharmacists. Invite them to walk with you during events, introducing the younger individual to pharmacists you know.

She also advises pharmacists to "Pick someone to mentor. Watch over them and encourage them. Likewise, a student or new pharmacist should look for someone to mentor them. It works both ways." Best of all, remember that pharmacy is a small world. You never know when a previous contact will be the person who can answer your question or help you out.

Metta Lou Henderson

A loyal friend laughs at your jokes
when they're not so good, and
sympathizes with your problems
when they're not so bad.

Arnold Glasow

 **TIP # 66**

Visit the Pharmacist.com
MTM Resource Center

Pharmacist.com has a rich MTM resource center full of tips, tools, and documents pharmacists can pull from to craft their practices. The site features a new MTM tip each month as well as continuing education related to MTM services. You can download MTM conference presentations as well. Subjects range from creating a business plan to certificate programs.

Marsha K. Millonig

 **TIP # 67**

Expand MTM Services to Assisted Living Facilities

David Zimmerman recommends that independent pharmacists explore the possibility of expanding their MTM services practices into assisted living facilities and skilled nursing homes. He advises starting with a local assisted living facility, and expanding from there. Assisted living is really an extension of retail practice, but follows many of the skilled nursing facility guidelines. These facilities are very demanding and provide pharmacists with opportunities to provide comprehensive services.

Numerous educational programs exist to help pharmacists with long-term care. David has taken many of these courses and found them extremely helpful.

David N. Zimmerman

 **TIP # 68**

Explain MTM to Patients

Just because patients can receive MTM services doesn't mean they'll come to visit you. "It's marketing and sales until you get them in the office," says Steve Simenson. "And don't underestimate how much work it is to make people realize that MTM is good for their future health and outcomes."

To bring MTM patients into his pharmacy, Simenson has his staff contact potential beneficiaries by phone and letter. In the letter, they make sure to include the pharmacy's address and directions. If any of the pharmacy staff knows the beneficiary, or shares a mutual friend, that employee contacts the person. Otherwise, they work from lists provided to them by the prescription drug plans.

On the phone, it's important to explain the health importance of MTM. "It's a service that none of them have ever experienced before, so be prepared to go from A to Z," says Simenson.

Steven T. Simenson

 **TIP # 69**

Separate MTM from Other Pharmacy Service Marketing

MTM hasn't led to a dramatic increase in Goodrich Pharmacy's dispensing clientele. "Initially, I thought that would happen, but it hasn't," says Steve Simenson. "People choose their dispensing pharmacy for a lot of different reasons, primarily convenience and location. We have picked up some patients, though, because some people will use MTM as a criterion for order fulfillment."

Although MTM might bring some patients into the pharmacy, the best long-term strategy might be to disassociate MTM and dispensing services. "I don't want to make people think if they get MTM here they can't go to another pharmacy," says Simenson. "There's no reason I can't provide MTM to the Walgreens or CVS patient." He says Goodrich's future is serving the entire community's MTM clientele, regardless of where they get their prescriptions filled.

Steven T. Simenson

☞ TIP # 70

Trumpet Successes

Pharmacist Patty Kumbera finds a key way to motivate new pharmacists to offer MTM services and secure more employers and insurers to pay for them is to trumpet current successes. Outcomes Pharmaceutical Health Care regularly shares success stories through news releases, meeting presentations, employer visits, participation at other key forums, and their web site.

Patty Kumbera

The question isn't who is going to let me; it's who is going to stop me?
                                                        Ayn Rand

☞ TIP # 71

Use Technology to Connect with the Pharmacy's Patient Base

Most people never leave home without the safety of their cell phone, so phone alerts can drive compliance wherever the patient happens to be. For homebound patients, alerts can be sent to the home phone as well. Susan Torrico recommends that pharmacists send automated email to individual patients when a refill is due and to encourage them to use commercial refill services. You can customize messages to include the pharmacy name and phone number. Some systems allow phone messages to be sent to an entire group to announce important events, such as the dates and times when flu shots will be available, or to announce that you are planning a health fair and request RSVPs. Phone reminders just prior to the event will greatly increase attendance by those who signed up to attend. This service is similar to the phone reminders that we all come to expect from our doctor and dentist. Why can't pharmacists use the same proven concept, but automate it through technology?

Susan Torrico

NOTES

 **TIP # 72**

Be a Patient Advocate

Former Minnesota state pharmacy association executive and pharmacist Don Dee says pharmacists need to take every opportunity to serve as patient advocates. Recently, Don's insurance plan reduced the day's supply of his chronic medication from 90 to 30 days. Working with his pharmacist, he was able to get this reversed by explaining to his insurance company how a 90-day supply helped him be more compliant—especially since he splits the year between two homes.

Donald A. Dee

 **TIP # 73**

Educate the Public and Legislators

To support faster growth of pharmacist-provided MTM services, pharmacists need to educate the public and their legislators about services beyond traditional dispensing. Publicizing successes with Medicare Part D and other MTM programs is an important way to start. Invite your legislator to visit the pharmacy and walk him or her through a brown-bag or MTM assessment. Recruiting local officials to be part of your MTM programs is a great way to create advocates for pharmacist services.

Donna Cestone
David Schwed

Never doubt that a small group of thoughtful, committed citizens can change the world. Indeed it is the only thing that ever has.

Margaret Mead

 **TIP # 74**

Engage in Community Outreach

Offer to conduct drug therapy education programs at local churches, YMCAs, service organizations (Kiwanis, Rotary, Elks, etc.) or nonprofit support groups (Parkinson's, Alzheimer's, diabetes, etc.). Nursing homes and recreational centers are also good places to network. Often a physician is in attendance, providing a relationship-building opportunity. Consider inviting the media to the event. School and college groups, hospitals, and local, county, and state physician organizations are all potential supporters of MTM programs. Presenting to them and outlining programs is a great way to gain support.

William N. Tindall

 **TIP # 75**

Explain to Patients What You Are Trying to Do

Pharmacists can help position MTM services by explaining to patients what they are trying to do for them and what outcomes they can expect. Ray Marcrom tells his patients, "If you just want the medicines, I'll give them to you, but here's what I'm trying to do for you." He suggests pharmacists always advocate for the patient, whether they get paid or not. Pharmacists should not ask, "Why don't patients want what we have?" but rather "What do we have that patients need?"

Ray Marcrom

If you put everything off until you're sure of it, you'll never get anything done.

Norman Vincent Peale

 **TIP # 76**

Invite a Physician to a Pharmacy Meeting

Invite a physician to attend a state, county, or national pharmacy meeting so he or she can find out just how much change has occurred in the pharmacy profession in the area of patient care. There is a lack of educational programs that encourage and showcase health professionals working together. This can address the problem.

William N. Tindall

 **TIP # 77**

Never Miss an Opportunity to Show What You Can Do

Consumer Stan Simmons says pharmacists should never miss an opportunity to show patients what you can do for them. For example, his daughter has allergies and is an avid sportsperson. Stan often picks up her medications. The pharmacist explained that the medicines might make his daughter tired at first, and also counseled about drug interactions. Stan was pleasantly surprised. "I had no idea about the medication's risks but was so pleased that the pharmacist took the time to talk with me. I now go to this pharmacy all the time and we have a great relationship."

Stan Simmons

NOTES

Continuing Professional Education and Skills Development

Avail Yourself of Free Resources

The pharmaceutical industry offers support for numerous continuing education and training programs. Often national meetings have pre- and post-meeting symposia. Stretch your development dollars further by taking advantage of these free resources to build your knowledge base.

Donna Cestone
David Schwed

 **TIP # 79**

Develop Confidence

One of the biggest barriers to providing MTM services is the pharmacist's lack of confidence to sit down with patients and dialogue with them on disease issues, observes Jeffrey Brewer. In many cases, pharmacists have the knowledge but believe they are out of practice. At his institution, they use role playing, case presentations, and mentoring to increase confidence and expand the number of pharmacists providing MTM services.

Jeffrey M. Brewer

Remember when you were at your best? Now be there again!
William Patterson

 TIP # 80

Know It's Never Too Late to Change

After graduating with a BPharm, Maria Maniscalco-Feichtl practiced in a supermarket pharmacy. Although she had worked in a community pharmacy for many years and had amazing mentors, she wanted more from the profession. She enrolled in a post-baccalau-reate PharmD program. Many of her peers questioned her decision to invest the time and money in an advanced degree, believing it would have no impact on her salary. She has found that decision and her subsequent residency training to be personal career highlights.

She currently provides both traditional order fulfillment and dispensing services in a community pharmacy environment, but also is a clinical service provider. Along with a team of pharmacists, she provides MTM services to patients by appointment. She considers herself a patient care generalist, yet she may address numerous diseases and conditions in any given day, including diabetes, hypertension, dyslipidemia, osteoporosis, asthma, chronic obstructive pulmonary disease, and smoking cessation. Appointments are scheduled from 15 minutes to one hour and patients pay a fee-for-service. The pharmacy director has also contracted with two local third-party payers to bill and receive payment for MTM services. "It is an exciting time for a pharmacist in practice," she notes.

The turning point in her professional outlook occurred when she realized—before attaining her doctorate—that she was providing MTM services. It is Maria's belief the typical community pharmacist does not realize he or she is *already* providing MTM services by addressing patients' concerns and requests and reviewing medication profiles. Often, the only missing elements are documentation and payment for the service. While practicing pharmacists like Maria may feel they need additional training to provide comprehensive MTM services, many active community pharmacists are set to go. All they may need is training in how to document and bill for their services. With the Medicare Part D MTM services and other third-party payers recognizing the pharmacist—not pharmacy—as the provider, a new paradigm has developed: compensation for pharmacist-provided cognitive services. "The time for a change in how we practice is now," she says.

Attaining the doctorate and completing a residency were key components for Maria's present ability to envision how community pharmacists can and should practice—not settling for the comfort zone of traditional dispensing. She believes community pharmacy practice is at a crossroad and that the agent for change is the community pharmacist. She encourages each pharmacist to get started implementing MTM services.

Maria Maniscalco-Feichtl

Throughout the centuries there were men who took first steps, down new roads, armed with nothing but their own vision.

Ayn Rand

TIP # 81

Keep Learning

Pharmacist John Hunter graduated long before MTM services were defined and implemented. Approaching retirement in a decade, he has become a leading provider of diabetes care for the pharmacy chain where he practices. How? He never stops learning and has taken advantage of a number of clinical issue forums held by the APhA Foundation. His advice to others is to "bite off more than you can chew" and never, ever stop learning and staying abreast of what is developing in the profession.

John Hunter

TIP # 82

Know Clinical Guidelines

Good patient care follows accepted clinical guidelines. Guidelines change, however.
An easy way to keep up is to regularly visit the National Guideline Clearinghouse (NGC), a public resource for evidence-based clinical practice guidelines at http://www.guideline.gov/.

NGC is an initiative of the Agency for Healthcare Research and Quality (AHRQ), U.S. Department of Health and Human Services. NGC was originally created by AHRQ in partnership with the American Medical Association and the American Association of Health Plans (now America's Health Insurance Plans [AHIP]). Click on "About NGC" to learn more.

Marsha K. Millonig

If you can find a path with no obstacles, it probably doesn't lead anywhere.
Frank A. Clark

☞ TIP # 83

Stay Up on Expanding Medical Literature

Jeffrey Brewer says it is challenging to stay up on rapidly expanding medical literature. He recommends several services that digest the primary literature and news for practitioners. One example is *The Pharmacist's Letter*. He suggests that pharmacists sign up online for the electronic table of contents of journals of interest. Many of the top journals make this easy to do on their web sites. Another option is to divide journals between the pharmacy staff and have each staff member create a monthly abstract of a topic of interest. This shared intelligence allows you to cover much more information.

Jeffrey M. Brewer

 # TIP # 84

Train Pharmacy Staff

Judy Sommers Hanson advises pharmacists to spend time training staff, including themselves. When staff members understand MTM services, they can provide better service.

Judith B. Sommers Hanson

 **TIP # 85**

Volunteer on Medication-Related Committees

Pharmacists should try to work jointly with colleagues on committees and projects that investigate drug therapy issues such as consumer education, treatment adherence, formularies, practice guidelines, and clinical trials.

William N. Tindall

If it doesn't absorb you, if it isn't any fun, don't do it.

D.H. Lawrence

NOTES

 **TIP # 86**

Ask the Right Question

Rachel Naomi Remen, physician, author and teacher of the course, "The Healer's Art," recalled aspects of her father's practice as a community pharmacist in New York City in the 1940s and 1950s. One particular question that he asked his patients was remarkably "clinical" in its character and simple in its delivery.
He would ask, "Is there anything about this medication that causes you concern?"
In answering, his patients were given the opportunity to reveal side effects, real or perceived impediments to adherence, and other factors that might potentially influence their outcomes from therapy. They also gained the benefit of realizing that their pharmacist was a caring professional.

Lucinda L. Maine

The responsibility of leadership is one of shaping our own and others' lives, hopefully for the better.

Delorese Ambrose

 **TIP # 87**

Become a Resource for Patients about Effective Compliance Tools

Most patients have no idea that compliance tools can help them manage their medications. They may need medication reminders but would not think to ask about them. Pharmacists are in a unique position to make a difference in the lives of patients or caregivers by simply providing useful information about available compliance tools. Susan Torrico encourages pharmacists to stay up on new products and services through their professional journals, magazines, and Internet resources.

Susan Torrico

 **TIP # 88**

Follow These Communication Pearls

Melissa Somma McGivney offers these communication pearls: welcome the patient and stay focused on him or her. Use nonverbal communication and an expressive tone of voice. Listen to the patient. Empower the patient and ensure follow up.

Melissa A. Somma McGivney

 **TIP # 89**

Listen

Learn from your patients. Give them adequate time to tell their story. Listening is the foundation to building relationships.

Heather Sakely

If a window of opportunity appears, don't pull down the shade.

Tom Peters

 **TIP # 90**

Encourage Your Patients to Carry Medication Lists

Medication wallet cards can be a useful tool for doctor and pharmacy visits and also in the event of an emergency. Encourage your patients to carry a wallet card that lists all the medications they take, including the name, strength, and dosage instructions. Wallet cards usually have space for the patient's current health conditions, advance directives, questions to ask caregivers, immunization information, and contact information for physicians and pharmacists. A number of wallet cards are available without charge via the Internet.

The Joint Commission, with the Centers for Medicare and Medicaid Services (CMS), launched a national campaign to urge patients to take a role in preventing health care errors by becoming active, involved, and informed participants on the health care team.

The program features brochures, posters and buttons on a variety of patient safety topics, including wallet cards. See http://www.joint-commission.org/PatientSafety/SpeakUp/speak_up_med_mistakes.htm for more information. The Iowa Healthcare Collaborative, in partnership with several hospitals and the Iowa Pharmacy Association, also makes a PDF wallet card available at http://www.ihconline.org/patients/patients.cfm. APhA's MTM resources and manuals also have templates for creating a patient's personal medication record. Finally, the National Council on Patient Information and Education has a wallet card available for purchase and numerous other patient resources on the web site www.talkaboutrx.org.

Marsha K. Millonig

☞ TIP # 91

Introduce Yourself

Patient care services provided by any health professional begin with a relationship. Most patients know their physician, dentist, and even veterinarian. But do patients often know their pharmacist's name? Be sure to introduce yourself. When patients get to know you, they are more likely to share information about their care with you.

Melissa A. Somma McGivney

☞ TIP # 92

Provide Quick Consults on Key Information

Studies routinely reported in the literature show that many patients who are prescribed anti-depressant medications, including SSRIs and SNRIs, take them for less than 6 to 8 weeks—the length of time it actually takes these medications to produce a therapeutic effect. In my experiences as a relief pharmacist in more than 30 pharmacies in my hometown, the literature was borne out. While I should not have been surprised, it was striking how many people were missing the opportunity to get better.

I decided one way to address the issue was to provide each patient who had a new prescription for an antidepressant with a quick consult when they picked up their prescription. My key message was: "this medicine may take up to 6 to 8 weeks to work." I created a brief list of these medicines. At each pharmacy I worked at that month, I talked with the pharmacy technicians, provided a copy of the medication list, and had them flag the finished prescriptions for these products with the "quick consult" tag. Patients were very appreciative and in most cases, did not realize how long it might take the medicine to work.

Marsha K. Millonig

The greatest tragedy is indifference.
The Red Cross

 # TIP # 93

Counsel Patients on Safety

Working in a retail pharmacy setting for eighteen years, pharmacy technician Lori Steinemann has seen many changes in community pharmacy practice. Some of the biggest changes include the growth of mail order and limited opportunities to go outside of the U.S. to save money. She says, "While you may not be able to persuade patients not to import medicines, you can help them reduce the safety risks associated with the practice." While talking with a good friend about his many medications and their costs, Lori was asked about prices at the pharmacy where she works. Lori researched the prices and got back to her friend. He explained that he was getting a couple (not all) of his prescriptions filled through the Internet from Canada, at a large savings. He asked her opinion on the matter. Lori told him that she understood and could sympathize with him on the cost issue, but was concerned about safety. She encouraged him to be forthcoming with his "Canadian pharmacist" as well as his local community pharmacist about all the medications he was taking. She stressed how important it was that they both know this information so they could check for drug interactions and side effects. She also advised him to tell his physician, especially in the event his medications were not working. They talked about the need to double check all medicines ordered online to ensure the drug looked the same, and to make sure that both his name and the name of the medication were on the container before taking any.

Lori Steinemann

☞ TIP # 94

Use Resources

Many pharmaceutical companies distribute marketing materials that include patient education information and helpful teaching aids. During her residency, Kristin Ball participated in various health fairs. Drug representatives were often present and they brought along many resources. At these venues, she would always look for those representatives with gadgets that her patients could benefit from—for example, large pill boxes which are especially good for HIV patients, and smaller ones that can fit in a purse. Pedometers, exercise videotapes for patients with diabetes, portion plates for teaching patients how to plan meals, and patient education materials (most available in English and Spanish) are some of the very useful tools Kristin has collected and used. She advises introducing yourself to the representative (or contacting the local sales representative in your area), explaining what you do, and asking them to mail you any available gadgets and other resources. In turn, she distributes them free to her patients.

Kristin N. Ball

MTM Models and Resources

TIP # 95

Address Lipid Therapy, Polypharmacy, and Medication Reconciliation All in One Clinic Visit

During her pharmacy practice residency, Mary Choy implemented a lipid clinic. Her initial goal was to manage patients' lipid medications by recommending appropriate medications, dosage adjustments, and discontinuations based on laboratory exam review.

With a click of the mouse, the computerized patient record system in the hospital provided access to patient progress notes, medication profiles, and laboratory exams. Given the hospital's primarily geriatric patient population, it was no surprise that each patient had 10+ medications at their initial visit. Mary reviewed their medication profiles and noticed that in many cases 1 to 2 medications could be discontinued to improve patient compliance and reduce the co-payment. This contributed to her goal of increasing medication cost-effectiveness as well.

In addition to addressing polypharmacy, Mary counseled patients on their other disease states and medications. Patients were especially thankful to have a current medication list noting reasons for each medicine's use. Many times, patients did not realize that stopping medications could lead to serious consequences.

As a result of her efforts, she extended patient visits from her original plan of 30 minutes to a full hour so she could address all issues. The clinic visits allowed patients to walk away with a better understanding of their disease states and lifestyle modifications, a streamlined medication regimen, and an overall appreciation for the pharmacist.

Mary Choy

Be great in act, as you have been in thought.

William Shakespeare

TIP # 96

Implement MTM Services:
El Rio Clinical Services Program

In Arizona, legislation passed (Arizona Revised Statute 32-1970) that allows qualified pharmacists in specified health care settings (such as a community health center) to implement, monitor, and modify drug therapy in collaboration with physicians according to written protocols. This practice model is referred to as collaborative drug therapy management (CDTM). El Rio has two of these sites. Focusing on disease state management, the clinical pharmacists make recommendations and changes in patient regimens.

The clinical pharmacist's responsibilities include coordinating care of patients with diabetes and common co-morbid disease states such as hypertension and dyslipidemia. In addition, the pharmacist is responsible for modification of drug therapy, measurement of blood glucose, Hemoglobin A1C levels, education of patients, and identification and resolution of compliance and therapy-related problems.

The largest portion of the pharmacist's work requires a comprehensive understanding of drug therapy, including formulary guidelines and drug protocols. Pharmacists must also continuously monitor labs to improve patient outcomes and identify actual or potential adverse drug reactions.

All interventions, pertinent lab data, patient demographics, and records of routine preventative therapy (i.e., monofilament exam, vaccinations, eye referrals, and podiatry referrals) are tracked via an Access® database. This database clearly and easily tracks each patient's progress in a consistent manner, reports clinic statistics in a timely fashion, and produces a progress note that is included in the patient's permanent medical record.

The pharmacist's involvement helps improve patients' quality of life, improve medication adherence, and avoid medication-related complications. Through the combined efforts of pharmacists and physicians, the health center has been able to integrate the two clinical pharmacists into El Rio's current treatment team, identify improvements in clinical outcomes of patients with diabetes and at the same time decrease costs, improve utilization of disease management services for patients with diabetes, and provide training to pharmacists in community health centers in Southern Arizona.

Sandra Leal

Note: The purpose of the HRSA demonstration projects was to examine the effects of expanded access to clinical pharmacists and comprehensive pharmacy services on the health outcomes of medically underserved populations. These reports evaluate expanded access and improved outcomes due to the clinical pharmacy demonstration projects. *Volume II: Case Studies* presents five case studies of clinical pharmacy demonstration project networks whose experience may prove beneficial to other community health centers and providers exploring the potential for clinical pharmacy service.

These resources provide more details about the El Rio program:

Leal S, Glover JJ, Herrier RN, Felix A. Improving quality of care in diabetes through a comprehensive pharmacist-based disease management program. *Diabetes Care* 2004; 27: 2983-4. Available at http://care.diabetes-journals.org/cgi/content/full/27/12/2983.

Leal S. Medications, rationing, and health care: the role of pharmacists in bridging the gap. *J Health Care Poor Underserved* 2005; 16(3): 418-420.

Leal S, Soto M. Pharmacists disease state management through a collaborative practice model. *J Health Care Poor Underserved* 2005; 16(2): 220-4.

Leal S. Changing the face of pharmacy. *Rx for Access* 2005. 2(5)2. MedPin.

Felt-Lisk S, Mays G, Harris L, Lee M, Nyman R, Smieliauskas F. Evaluation of HRSA's Clinical Pharmacy Demonstration Projects Final Report – Volume I: Synthesis Report. November 30, 2004. Available at ftp://ftp.hrsa.gov/bphc/pdf/opa/CPDPvolume1finalreport.pdf.

Felt-Lisk S, Harris L, Lee M, Nyman R. Evaluation of HRSA's Clinical Pharmacy Demonstration Projects Final Report – Volume II: Case Studies. November 30, 2004. Available at ftp://ftp.hrsa.gov/bphc/pdf/opa/CPDPvolume2finalreport.pdf.

 **TIP # 97**

Keep Up with MTM Developments

Pharmacist Daniel Touchette advises pharmacists to keep up with MTM service developments. He conducts research projects on various MTM service models and is working on a literature review of MTM service programs that will be published in a peer-reviewed journal. Staying abreast of MTM service developments through professional journals and meetings can be very helpful when developing an MTM services practice.

Daniel R. Touchette

Not everything that can be counted counts, and not everything that counts can be counted.
Albert Einstein

 **TIP # 98**

Implement a Pharmacy Outreach Program: MassMedLine MTM Practice

"We are everyday pharmacists in a slightly different role," says Mary Sullivan of the MassMedLine practice. MassMedLine is a pharmacy outreach program run through the Massachusetts College of Pharmacy and Health Sciences as a public service to the people of the Commonwealth of Massachusetts. MassMedLine ensures medication compliance and adherence through medication management and cost-saving programs. This includes federal, state, and private programs. Residents of Massachusetts reach MassMedLine either through a toll-free Massachusetts help line or through the walk-in center.

MassMedLine's case managers assess patients for eligibility for various programs and assist them with the enrollment process, including the Medicare drug benefit and patient assistance programs offered through the pharmaceutical industry. Each patient who calls for help is also contacted by a pharmacist to review medication-related issues.

In conjunction with Massachusetts College of Pharmacy and Health Sciences' Center for Drug Information and Natural Products, MassMedLine pharmacists provide a comprehensive, standardized MTM evaluation, including:

- Interviewing and counseling patients.
- Providing any needed assistance.
- Providing simple, easy-to-read correspondence.
- Discussing medication profiles in detail, including any areas where alterations or alternatives may be necessary.
- Giving patients an easy-to-understand pharmacist recommendation form for discussion and physician review.
- Notifying physicians regarding recommendations when necessary.

Follow-up calls or visits are scheduled for one month from the last consult to ensure that questions were answered and new medications and issues are reviewed.

Mary Sullivan
Paula Evans
Donna Bartlett

*Small opportunities are often the
beginning of great enterprises.*

Demosthenes

 **TIP # 99**

Create and Implement a Neurological Pharmacist MTM Service

There are many opportunities for pharmacists to intervene on behalf of patients with neurological disorders and to gain reimbursement for these services. Ruth Nemire works specifically with patients who have seizures and epilepsy. Patients with epilepsy usually access medical care for treatment of their seizures either emergently in status epilepticus, emergently not in status, or as ambulatory patients in the clinic or physician's office.

Because they lack understanding of epilepsy and seizures, many patients find themselves in the emergency room (ER) after being transported by an ambulance against their will and/or without their knowledge because of one seizure. Many times these patients are treated in the ER based on their drug levels and are subsequently prescribed an increase of medication dosage without a good review of recent history by the treating health care provider. Often these changes interfere with treatment plans of the patient's primary care physician, epileptologist, or follow-up care pharmacist.

Pharmacists can play a key role in developing and participating in a status epilepticus team. The presence of such teams can make as much of a difference in the outcome of status as the drug that is chosen. Hospital pharmacists can complete histories and work with ER physicians to make sure that the patient's care doesn't take a step backwards when he or she lands in the hospital due to a seizure. These services are billable by the pharmacist.

Ruth has been part of a health care team in a university medical center and an epilepsy foundation clinic. The pharmacist's role in each of these clinics varies. Based on her experience, Ruth advises pharmacists to:

- Conduct a good review of the patient's past medical history to determine diagnosis and treatment of epilepsy and other neurological diseases.
- Review records and obtain the patient history including chief complaint, medical history, family and social history, current illness, treatment, previous response to therapies, adverse reactions, and allergy information prior to initial visits.
- Participate in developing a therapeutic plan once a diagnosis is made or confirmed.
- Provide follow-up care for patients, including a history, review of the current illness, and a brief physical assessment to assess adverse effects.
- Recommend continued treatment or alter the therapeutic plan, and provide prescriptions and other medication-related directions to the patient.

Pharmacists in these clinics are also aware of the social and psychological aspects of the patient's circumstances and participate in making sure patients can manage the medication therapy plan, including medication access.

These pharmacist-provided services have been billed and reimbursed through Medicaid or grant programs.

Ruth E. Nemire

*When you hold back on life,
life holds back on you.*
                    Mary Manin Morrissey

 # TIP # 100

Use a Team Approach to Implement an MTM Service: University of Georgia College of Pharmacy/Kroger Pharmacy

A team of pharmacists at the University of Georgia College of Pharmacy wanted to develop an MTM services program to take advantage of Medicare Part D. To begin, they obtained contact information from the APhA MTM Resource Center web site for Medicare Part D sponsors. After contacting them, five plans (WellCare, RxAmerica, Instil, CIGNA, and

Aetna) informed the team that they could start outsourcing MTM services.

The group then decided to design and test a community pharmacy model for implementing and conducting MTM services that they could duplicate in various community settings. Eligible participants were persons 18 and older who take more than three medications a day. The team created forms to gather patient information, document recommendations, and communicate with physicians. They recruited patients using overhead announcements, in-store flyers, and prescription bag stuffers. Interested patients made appointments and completed patient information forms prior to their appointments. Participants' primary care physicians were then contacted to obtain laboratory values. During and directly following the MTM session, the team documented any issues identified along with any recommendations on the corresponding forms. After their session, a ten-item survey was administered to patients to determine patient acceptance and willingness to pay.

As of February 2007, patient response had been promising. The majority of patients were recruited by prescription bag stuffers and the team had not received any complaints from participants regarding the required forms. Patients sign a consent form allowing pharmacists to contact their primary care physician to obtain recent laboratory values. The consent form, along with a letter of request, is sent to the physician via facsimile a week before the appointment. The response from the physicians was surprising for the group; they were able to obtain laboratory values for every patient seen.

One challenge has been the time commitment required not only to conduct the MTM sessions but to document the appropriate information. In addition to the half-hour spent with each patient, reviewing patient information prior to the appointment can take up to an hour per patient depending on the extent of his or her conditions, and the team can spend an additional hour documenting the session and following up with the patient.

Currently, the group is documenting everything in paper charts, which is time-consuming. Appropriate use of available technology, such as electronic charting systems, could potentially save time, increase efficiency, and aid in the billing process. Once the study has been completed, the group plans to analyze the data collected and publish the results.

Brian D. Buck
Landon Castleman
Patricia Powell

Index

H

I

J

K

L

N

O

P

T

W

Z